GET ACTIVE!

I0895108

BUILDING ENDURANCE

Written by Valerie Harvey

KidHaven PUBLISHING

Published in 2027 by
KidHaven Publishing, an Imprint of Greenhaven Publishing, LLC
2544 Clinton St., Buffalo, NY 14224

Written by: Valerie Harvey
Edited by: Elise Carraway
Designed by: Jasmine Pointer

All facts, statistics, web addresses, and URLs in this book were verified as valid and accurate at time of writing. No responsibility for any changes to external websites or references can be accepted by either the author or publisher.

Cataloging-in-Publication Data

Names: Harvey, Valerie.
Title: Building endurance / Valerie Harvey.
Description: Buffalo, NY : KidHaven Publishing, 2027. | Series: Get active! | Includes glossary and index.
Identifiers: ISBN 9781534570764 (pbk.) | ISBN 9781534570771 (library bound) | ISBN 9781534570788 (ebook)
Subjects: LCSH: Physical fitness--Juvenile literature. | Aerobic exercises--Juvenile literature.
Classification: LCC GV481.H378 2027 | DDC 613.7--dc23

Printed in China

CPSIA compliance information: Batch #QS27KH: For further information contact Greenhaven Publishing LLC at 1-844-317-7404.

Please visit our website, www.greenhavenpublishing.com.
For a free color catalog of all our high-quality books, call toll free 1-844-317-7404 or fax 1-844-317-7405.

Find us on

Image Credits. All images are courtesy of Shutterstock.com, unless otherwise stated.

Recurring – Tatiana Kubara, VVadi4ka. Cover – suriyachan. 2–3 – PeopleImages. 4–5 – Ground Picture, Oleg Mikhaylov. 6–7 – Zamrznuti tonovi, PeopleImages. 8–9 – PeopleImages. 10–11 – TinnaPong, Rawpixel.com. 12–13 – Richard Rolanda, Rawpixel.com. 14–15 – Gorodenkoff, mTaira. 16–17 – PeopleImages, pics five. 18–19 – Ground Picture, BearFotos. 20–21 – Lopolo, Volodymyr TVERDOKHLIB. 22–23 – LightField Studios, Prostock-studio.

CONTENTS

Words that look like this can be found in the glossary on page 24.

Let's GET ACTIVE!

Are you full of <u>energy</u>? There are lots of ways that you can get active and get your body moving. You could play sports, go for a run, or dance around.

It is important to care for your body. Getting active needs endurance, so keeping your muscles strong and healthy can really help you stay active for longer. Let's get your body moving!

WHAT IS ENDURANCE?

Endurance means being able to keep going, even when something is hard or takes a long time. In sports, endurance helps you run, swim, or play for a long time without getting too tired.

It is like being a superhero who does not give up! Athletes build endurance by practicing a lot, staying strong, and believing in themselves—even when their bodies feel tired.

HEART RATE

Your heart rate is how fast your heart is beating. When sitting still, most adults' hearts beat 60 to 100 times in 1 minute. A child's heart rate might be similar or just a little bit higher.

Have you ever felt your own heartbeat?

Your heart pumps blood and oxygen around your body. When you exercise, your heart beats faster. This is because your muscles need more oxygen to help them stay active.

ENERGY

Your body needs energy to run, jump, and play for a long time. Energy helps your heart and other muscles keep going. When you run out of energy, your body might feel slow, heavy, and tired.

We get energy from foods that contain carbohydrates, such as bread, pasta, and rice. When you eat a healthy balance of foods, your body has the power to play longer and feel strong!

HYDRATION

Hydration means drinking enough water to help your body stay cool and healthy. When you exercise, you might end up sweating. That means your body loses water. It is important to stay hydrated.

When exercising, it is important to take sips often instead of just drinking a lot at once. This is what athletes do. Athletes drink water to keep their energy up and perform at their best.

MENTAL ENDURANCE

Mental endurance means carrying on and staying focused even when things get tough. Some sports and activities can be a big challenge, such as running a marathon. It takes mental endurance to get through them.

Mental endurance also helps when losing in sports. Part of being a good athlete is being able to keep going even if you are losing.

Athletes need the mental endurance to keep going even if it feels like they have already given everything they have.

MOTIVATION

Motivation is the feeling of wanting to do something. Different things might motivate different people to keep going when it gets hard. For some people, just wanting to have fun is enough motivation to be active. Others want to get better at a sport so that they can win.

The thought of getting better motivates some athletes. They might want to improve their endurance when they run or swim. They might want to get stronger and lift heavier things for longer.

BUILDING ENDURANCE

You can build endurance by practicing a little bit every day. Try playing or walking for a few minutes, then each day do it for a bit longer. See if you can keep going.

Remember to eat enough, drink water, and get plenty of sleep so your body feels strong. The more you practice and the better you take care of your body, the longer you can stay active.

MEASURING PROGRESS

You can see if your endurance gets better by keeping track of your active time. You could see how far you go or how long you stay active.

You can set little goals, such as running a bit faster or biking a little farther each week. When you meet your goals, it shows that your body is getting stronger and your endurance is improving!

ENDURANCE ENDEAVORS

Having good endurance is very helpful. It can help you in everyday life. Endurance can help you play for longer and help you get through long days.

Athletes use their endurance to keep going when things get tough. It helps them to get over the finish line and win races. What can you do with your endurance?

GLOSSARY

ATHLETES people who are skilled at sports

CARBOHYDRATES sugars inside food that our bodies break down and turn into energy

ENERGY the power that makes living things able to move and live

MARATHON a really long running race

MUSCLES the parts of the body that help it move

OXYGEN a natural gas that living things need in order to survive

INDEX